AN ALPHABET OF ANIMALS

A

B

C

D

E

F

G

H

I

J

K

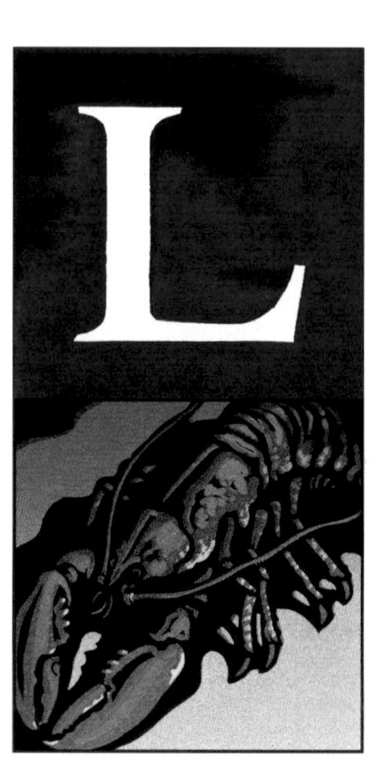
L

M

N

O

P

Q

R

S

T

U

V

W

X

Y

Z

AN ALPHABET OF ANIMALS

BY CHRISTOPHER WORMELL

COLLINS

William Collins Sons & Co Ltd
London · Glasgow · Sydney · Auckland
Toronto · Johannesburg

First published 1990

A CIP catalogue record for this book is available from the British Library

ISBN 0 00 191378 6

Printed in Belgium by
Proost International Book Productions

The art for this book was created from hand cut lino block prints. Several blocks (generally four) were cut for each picture. Each block was inked with a roller and printed separately by hand, producing the black images and the colour areas. In certain instances, to achieve a shading or blending of colours, more than one colour ink was applied to the same block. All of the art was colour-separated by scanner and reproduced in full colour.

For Jack

Aa

Alligator

B b

Bear

Cc

Cobra

Dd

Donkey

Ee

Elephant

Ff

Frog

Gg

Goose

Hh

Hippopotamus

I i

Iguana

J j

Jackal

Kk

Kangaroo

L l

Lobster

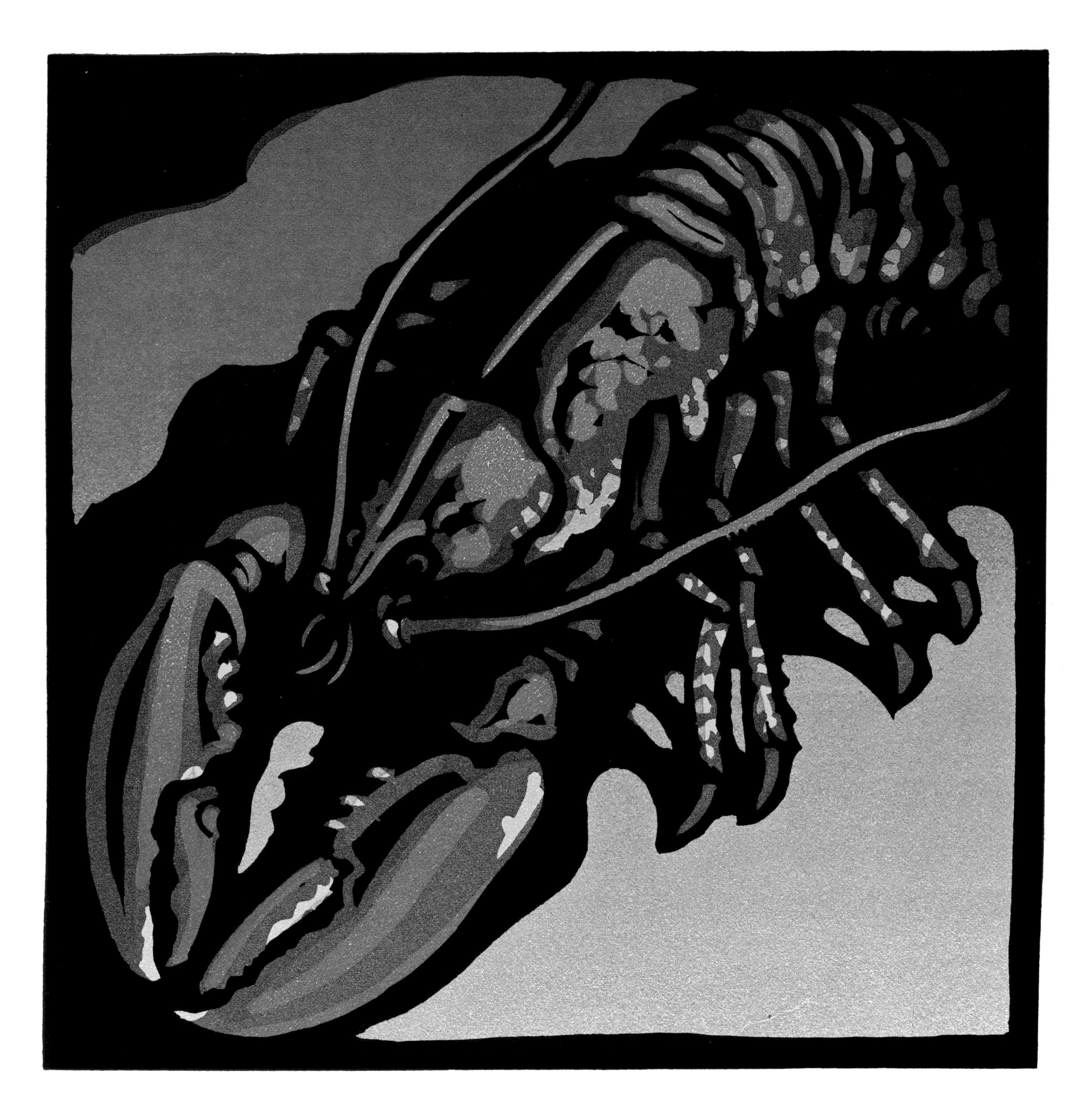

Mm

Moose

Nn

Narwhal

Oo

Orang-utan

Pp

Pig

Q q

Quetzal

Rr

Rooster

Ss

Swan

Tt

Tiger

U u

Umbrella Bird

Vv

Vulture

Ww

Walrus

Xx

Xenops

Y y

Yak

Zz

Zebra

SOME OF THE LESS FAMILIAR ANIMALS FEATURED IN THIS BOOK INCLUDE:

IGUANA A large tropical lizard found in Central America, South America, and southern North America.

JACKAL A mammal related to the dog and wolf, found in Africa and southern Asia, where it inhabits deserts, grasslands, and brush country.

NARWHAL A small whale found in the Arctic and North Atlantic oceans. The male narwhal has a single, tightly spiralled tusk.

QUETZAL A bird found in rain forests from southern Mexico through Central America, at altitudes of up to 9000 feet.

UMBRELLA BIRD Found from Central America to northern South America, where it inhabits forest tree tops.

XENOPS A small kind of ovenbird, found in parts of Central and South America.

YAK A large long-haired ox found in Tibet and other high-altitude regions of central Asia.

Christopher Wormell, now established as one of the leading English wood engravers, surprisingly has never illustrated a children's book. Inspired by the works of Thomas Bewick he took up wood engraving in 1982. Though originally attracted to the medium as the ideal way to illustrate books, he has since found most of his commissions both in the UK and abroad in the field of advertising and design, where wood engraving has in recent years enjoyed something of a boom.

Long before Christopher became a wood engraver he was taught lino-cutting by his father, mainly for the mass production of Christmas cards. Around Christmas time the Wormell household became something of a cottage industry with Christopher and his brothers and sisters producing handmade cards by the hundred.

Christopher returned to lino-cutting to make simple, colourful pictures for his own son Jack and the idea soon developed into this, his first book for children.

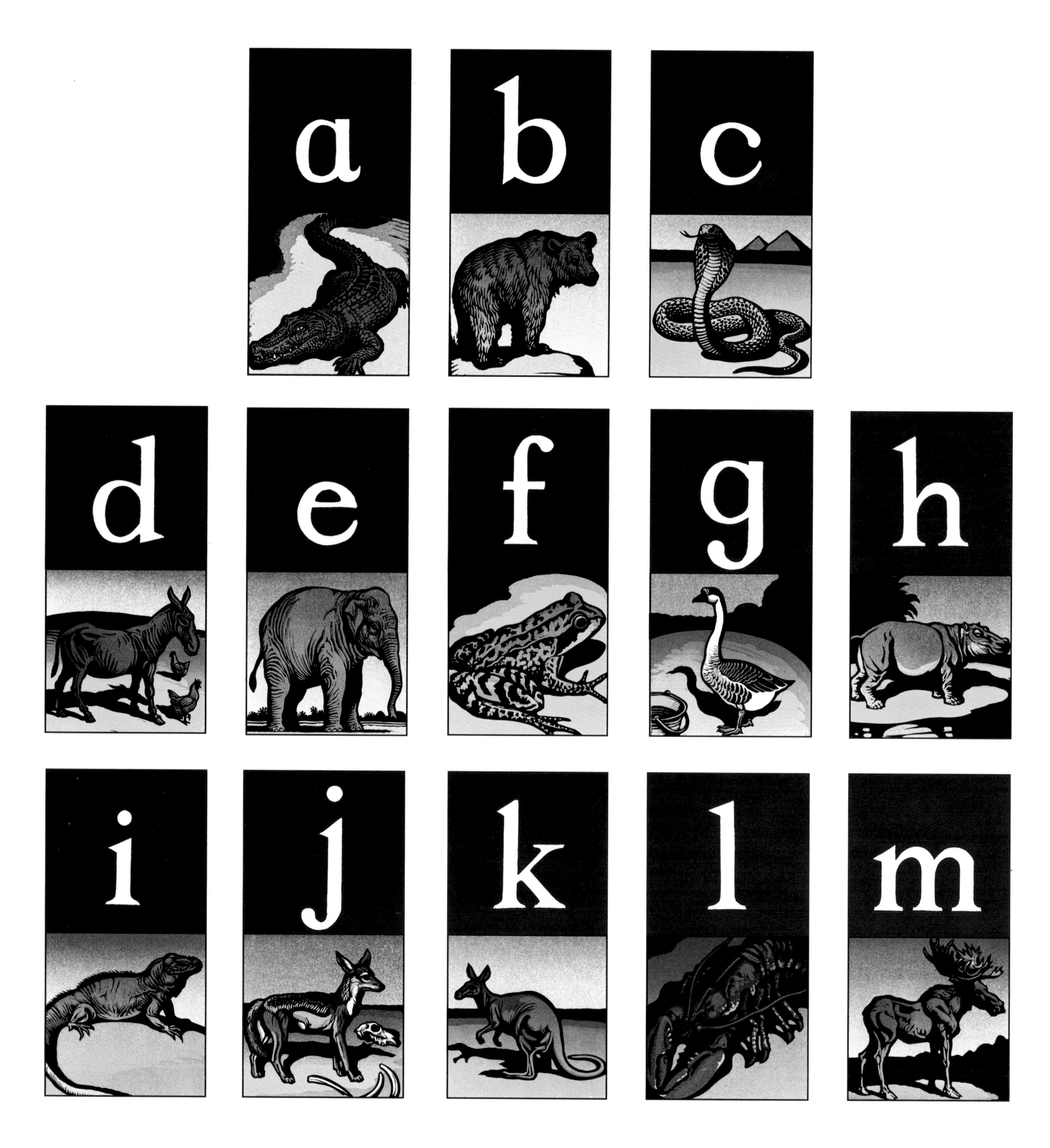
a
b
c
d
e
f
g
h
i
j
k
l
m

x